Algebra
Quick Starts

Author: Wendi Silvano
Editor: Mary Dieterich
Proofreaders: April Albert and Margaret Brown

COPYRIGHT © 2018 Mark Twain Media, Inc.

ISBN 978-1-62223-697-8

Printing No. CD-405020

Mark Twain Media, Inc., Publishers
Distributed by Carson-Dellosa Publishing LLC

Table of Contents

Introduction to the Teacher

It is important for students to review and practice the skills they gain as they learn algebra. Revisiting math skills several days after they are first learned is a helpful way to reinforce those skills.

This book is intended to offer the teacher and parent short quick-start activities to help the student practice the skills that are taught in the classroom. Each mini-activity can be used at the beginning of class to help students focus on algebra for the day. The activities can also be used as a review before testing, or they can be kept in a learning center for students to complete when they have extra time. The activities use all of the basic skills of algebra from real numbers to quadratic equations.

Each page may be copied and cut apart, so that the individual sections can be used as quick starts for each day of the week. The teacher could also give each student the entire page to keep in a three-ring binder to use as assigned. Another option would be to make a transparency of the page to be done as whole-class activities or for the students to copy. Please be aware that students will need scratch paper to complete some of the quick starts.

Real Numbers

Real Numbers 1

Give the coordinate of each point on the number line.

A. _____   B. _____   C. _____   D. _____

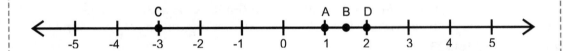

Real Numbers 2

Graph these numbers on the number line.

A. (-3)   B. $(+3\frac{1}{2})$ C. (-4.5)   D. $(+\frac{1}{4})$

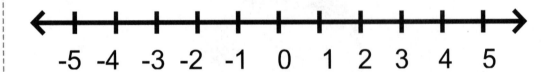

Real Numbers 3

Place >, <, or = on each line to make each statement true.

a. -2 _____ 4   b. 5.38 _____ 5.3

c. $1\frac{1}{2}$ _____ 1.5   d. -3.1 _____ -3.6

Real Numbers

Real Numbers 4

List each set of real numbers in order from least to greatest.

a. $(4, -2, -\frac{3}{4}, 1\frac{1}{3}, 0)$

_____

b. $(4.6, \sqrt{25}, -2.8, 4.10, -3)$

_____

Real Numbers 5

Simplify.

a. -(-4) _____

b. $(-[-(\frac{1}{5})])$ _____

c. | 16 | _____

d. | -9.1 | _____

Real Numbers 6

Find each difference.

a. -(16) – (-5) = _____

b. (-36) – (14) = _____

c. $\frac{2}{3} - (-\frac{1}{3})$ = _____

d. 16 – (-4) = _____

e. (3.5) – (-1.1) – (2.6) = _____

Real Numbers 7

Find each product.

a. (-4) (5) = _____

b. (12) (6) = _____

c. (2.1) (-4.3) = _____

d. $(-\frac{2}{3}) (-\frac{4}{5})$ _____

e. (3) (6) (-5) = _____

Real Numbers

Real Numbers 8

Find each quotient.

a. $-81 \div 3 =$ _____

b. $-\frac{36}{9} =$ _____

c. $-\frac{1}{2} \div (-\frac{2}{3}) =$ _____

d. $0 \div 116 =$ _____

e. $8.75 \div (-0.5) =$ _____

Real Numbers 9

Find each sum.

a. $-4 + 7 =$ _____

b. $-3 + (-4) =$ _____

c. $286 + (-153) =$ _____

d. $-622 + (-304) =$ _____

e. $(1.2) + (3.3) + (-1.6) =$ _____

f. $(-\frac{2}{5}) + (-\frac{1}{3}) + (\frac{3}{5}) =$ _____

Real Numbers 10

Find the difference.

In January, the average daily low temperature in Fairbanks, Alaska, is -18°F. In July, it is 52°F. How many degrees difference is there between the average daily low temperatures of January and July?

_____

Real Numbers 11

Mark *T* for true or *F* for false for each statement.

_____ a. $-6 + 4 = 4 + (-6)$

_____ b. $8 - 12 = 12 - 8$

_____ c. $6 + (14 - 8) =$
             $(6 + 14) - 8$

_____ d. $9 \div 3 = 3 \div 9$

_____ e. $2(3 + 5) = 2(3) + 2(5)$

Real Numbers

Real Numbers 12

Write the reciprocal of each number.

a. -3 _____

b. $\sqrt{21}$ _____

c. $\frac{3}{4}$ _____

d. -2 _____

e. $\frac{19}{8}$ _____

f. $\dfrac{12}{\sqrt{7}}$ _____

R
E
C
I
P
R
O
C
A
L

Real Numbers 13

Number these rules to show the order of operations.

_____ Evaluate expressions with exponents.

_____ Do all additions and subtractions in order from left to right.

_____ Do all operations within parentheses.

_____ Do all multiplications and divisions in order from left to right.

Real Numbers 14

Simplify.

a. $18 - 3 \cdot 4 + 6 \div 3$ _____

b. $3(2 + 5) - 2^2$ _____

c. $4(6 + 8 - 3 + 1)$ _____

Real Numbers 15

Simplify.

a. $\{20 - [3(1 + 3)]\} \cdot 2$ _____

b. $3^3 + (14 - 8) \cdot 2$ _____

c. $(4^2 + 2^2) \div 5$ _____

Algebraic Expressions

Algebraic Expressions 1

Evaluate each expression if $n = 12$.

a. $n + 15$ _____

b. $50 - n$ _____

c. $7n$ _____

d. $\dfrac{n}{4}$ _____

Algebraic Expressions 2

Evaluate each expression if $a = 3$, $b = 5$, and $c = 2$.

a. $3abc$ _____

b. $\dfrac{1}{2}a + b$ _____

c. b^c _____

Algebraic Expressions 3

Evaluate each expression if $p = \dfrac{1}{4}$ and $r = \dfrac{1}{2}$.

a. $p + r$ _____

b. $r - p$ _____

c. pr _____

d. $\dfrac{p}{r}$ _____

Algebraic Expressions 4

Write an algebraic expression that could answer each question if n is Dan's age now.

a. What was Dan's age 3 years ago?

   _____

b. What age will Dan be in 8 years?

   _____

c. How many years until Dan is 50?

   _____

Algebraic Expressions

Algebraic Expressions 5

Write an algebraic expression for each phrase.

a. Some number n increased by 8

_____

b. The difference of 12 and s

_____

c. Three less than 4 times a number t

_____

d. g divided by h

_____

Algebraic Expressions 6

Evaluate each expression if $x = 2$ and $y = 3$.

a. x^2y _____

b. x^3y^2 _____

c. $x^2 + y^2$ _____

d. $-(xy)^2$ _____

Algebraic Expressions 7

Evaluate each expression.

a. x^4 if $x = 2$ _____

b. r^3 if $r = 3$ _____

c. m^3 if $m = -1$ _____

d. $n^2 - n$ if $n = 4$ _____

Algebraic Expressions 8

Evaluate each expression if $a = 3$, $b = 4$, and $c = -2$.

a. $-b + c^2$ _____

b. $(c - a)^2$ _____

c. $a^2(b + c)^2$ _____

d. $-(3a + 2c)^3$ _____

Algebraic Expressions

Algebraic Expressions 9

Evaluate each expression if $x = 2$ and $y = -3$.

a. $x^2 + y^2 + 1$ _____

b. $2x^2 - 3x + 5$ _____

c. $3x^2 + 2y$ _____

d. $x^3 - 2y$ _____

Algebraic Expressions 10

Evaluate each expression if $a = -2$, $b = 6$, and $c = 4$.

a. $\dfrac{a^3 + c^2}{bc}$ _____

b. $-b + a^2(3c - a)$ _____

c. $b^2 \div (c^2 - a)$ _____

Algebraic Expressions 11

For each expression, tell whether the terms are *like* or *unlike*.

a. $4s + 8$ _____

b. $2a^2b + 3ab^2$ _____

c. $3xy^2 + 2xy^2$ _____

d. $2pq^2r - pq^2r$ _____

Algebraic Expressions 12

Write the coefficient of each term.

a. $6x^2$ _____

b. y _____

c. $5y^3$ _____

d. $10z^5$ _____

e. $18a^4b^2$ _____

Algebraic Expressions

Algebraic Expressions 13

Simplify.

a. $2n + 4n + 5n^2 + 3n^2$ _____

b. $5x^2y + 2x^2y - 3xy$ _____

c. $-6 + 3(2b - 4) + 3b$ _____

d. $4a^3b + 3ab^3 + 2a^3b + 6ab^3$ _____

Algebraic Expressions 14

Simplify.

a. $5(ab^2 - 2ab) + 3(ab - ab^2)$ _____

b. $\frac{1}{2}(4x + 2y) + \frac{1}{3}(12x - 6y)$ _____

c. $3(g^3 - h) + 4(g^3 - 8)$ _____

Algebraic Expressions 15

Simplify.

a. $2n + 4n$ _____ b. $-4y - 3y$ _____

c. $7 + 2t + 4$ _____ d. $12b^2 - 4b^2$ _____

e. $3(x + 4) - 6$ _____

f. $6x^3y - 3x^3y + 4xy$ _____

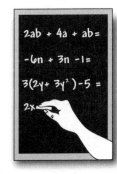

Algebraic Expressions

Algebraic Expressions 16

Translate each phrase into an algebraic expression. (Use *n* to represent a variable.)

a. Five more than three times a

number _____

b. Four times the sum of a number

and six _____

c. Two less than eight times a

number squared

_____

Algebraic Expressions 17

Write an algebraic expression for one unknown in terms of the other. (Use *g* to represent the girls and *b* to represent the boys.)

a. There are four more boys than girls in class.

_____

b. If the girls' team wins one more game, they will have won twice as many games as the boys.

_____

Algebraic Expressions 18

Find the solution set of each sentence. The replacement set is {-1,0,1}.

a. $k + 3 = 3$ _____

b. $m + 1 = 0$ _____

c. $y + 1 \leq 1$ _____

d. $2n > 2$ _____

Algebraic Expressions 19

a. A stereo costs $110. John paid $35 down and made 5 equal payments on the stereo. Write an algebraic equation that could be used to find out how much his payments were.

_____

b. Andrea's new coat costs $25 more than twice as much as her old one. The new coat costs $105. Write an algebraic equation that could be used to determine how much her old coat cost.

_____

Linear Equations & Inequalities

Linear Equations & Inequalities 1

Tell which operation you would perform on each side of the equation to get x alone on one side.

a. $x + 3 = 7$ _____

b. $-4 = -1 + x$ _____

c. $x - 6 = 10$ _____

d. $x - (-12) = 15$ _____

Linear Equations & Inequalities 2

Solve.

a. $a - 4 = 24$ _____

b. $m + 3 = 18$ _____

c. $r + 11 = 22$ _____

d. $12 + s = -10$ _____

Linear Equations & Inequalities 3

Solve.

a. $b - (-4) = 10$ _____

b. $-3.4 + r = -9.5$ _____

c. $5 = x + 2\frac{1}{3}$ _____

d. $b - 3.12 = 5.23$ _____

Linear Equations & Inequalities 4

Write and solve an algebraic equation to answer the following.

If a number n is decreased by 32, it equals 11. Find n.

_____

Linear Equations & Inequalities

Linear Equations & Inequalities 5

Is the given number a solution for the equation?

	Given Number	Equation	
a.	3	$x + 3 = 5$	_____
b.	2	$3y + 6 = 12$	_____
c.	-5	$\dfrac{3v - 5}{4} = -5$	_____

Linear Equations & Inequalities 6

Is the given number a solution for the equation?

	Given Number	Equation	
a.	5	$6x = 42$	_____
b.	7	$\dfrac{14}{b} = 2$	_____
c.	-3	$\dfrac{5m + 3}{6} = -2$	_____

Linear Equations & Inequalities 7

The formula to find the area of a triangle is $A = \frac{1}{2}bh$.

a. What is the area (A) if $b = 6$ and $h = 5$? _____

b. What is the height (h) if $b = 4$ and $A = 16$? _____

c. What is the base (b) if $h = 4$ and $A = 12$? _____

Linear Equations & Inequalities

Linear Equations & Inequalities 8

What must be done to each side of the equation so the variable will be alone on one side?

a. $6x = 42$

_____

b. $\frac{2}{3}m = 1$

_____

c. $-18 = -3y$

_____

Linear Equations & Inequalities 9

Solve.

a. $-5t = 30$ _____

b. $2x = 14$ _____

c. $\dfrac{x}{7} = -4$ _____

d. $\frac{3}{5}p = 12$ _____

Linear Equations & Inequalities 10

Solve.

a. $1.25x = 5$ _____

b. $\frac{2}{3}a = 4$ _____

c. $\dfrac{s}{5} = 10$ _____

d. $-3.5b = 14$ _____

Linear Equations & Inequalities 11

Write an algebraic equation for each word sentence and then solve.

a. The quotient of 30 and a number n equals 6.

_____

b. The product of 9 and a number c equals 27.

_____

Linear Equations & Inequalities

Linear Equations & Inequalities 12

Solve.

a. $4m + 8 = 20$ _____

b. $2x - 4 = 6$ _____

c. $b + 11 = 4$ _____

d. $\frac{2}{3}k + 7 = 13$ _____

Linear Equations & Inequalities 13

Solve.

a. $3(x - 4) = 12$ _____

b. $\frac{1}{4}(a - 16) = 16$ _____

c. $2y - 15 = -1$ _____

d. $\dfrac{2c - 6}{2} = 9$ _____

Linear Equations & Inequalities 14

Complete each sentence.

a. If $x + 7 = 9$, then $11 - x =$

_____

b. If $4y + 2 = 14$, then $2y + 1 =$

_____

c. If $3b + 4 = 19$, then $6b =$

_____

d. If $2c - 1 = 5$, then $c + 8 =$

_____

Linear Equations & Inequalities 15

Solve each problem by writing and solving an equation.

a. Ten less than three times x is 50. Find x.

_____

b. The sum of n and five times n equals 12.

_____

Linear Equations & Inequalities

Linear Equations & Inequalities 16

Solve. The circumference of a circle can be found with the formula $C = 2\pi r$.

a. Find C if $\pi = 3.14$ and $r = 10$.

_____

b. Find r if $C = 94.2$ and $\pi = 3.14$.

_____

Linear Equations & Inequalities 17

Use the distributive property to find each product.

a. $6(n - 4)$

_____

b. $(5 + d)3$

_____

c. $25(4 + 3s)$

_____

d. $3(a + b)$

_____

Linear Equations & Inequalities 18

Solve.

a. $a + (a + 4) + (2a - 3) = 13$

_____

b. $2(y - 3) = 12$

_____

c. $8(m - 1) = 8$

_____

d. $-2(4x - 3) = -14$

_____

Linear Equations & Inequalities 19

Solve.

a. What is 8% of 98?

_____

b. 6 is what percent of 24?

_____

c. 40% of what number is 60?

_____

d. What is 15.5% of 50?

_____

Linear Equations & Inequalities

Linear Equations & Inequalities 20

Solve.

a. $3a - 8 = -6 + a$ _____

b. $4x - 10 = x - 16$ _____

c. $-5b = 3(4 - 3b)$ _____

d. $2x + 4(x - 2) = -(2x - 8)$ _____

Linear Equations & Inequalities 21

Solve and state the solution set.

a. $|2a + 7| = 9$ _____   b. $|\frac{1}{3}b - 2| = 4$ _____

c. $|y - 4| > 6$ _____   d. $|2g - 9| \geq 1$ _____

Linear Equations & Inequalities 22

Circle the sentence that best describes the graph.

a. $x \geq -2$ b. $x = -2$ c. $x < -2$ d. $x > -2$ e. $x \leq -2$

Linear Equations & Inequalities

Linear Equations & Inequalities 23

Solve.

a. $2y - 1 = -3(2 + y)$ _____

b. $-3(x - 2) + 4 = 4(x + 1)$ _____

c. $5u - 14 = -5 + 8u$ _____

Linear Equations & Inequalities 24

Solve.

a. $4y + 6 < 2y - 6$ _____   b. $5x + 2 - 4x \geq 3$ _____

c. $8c < 56$ _____   d. $\frac{3}{4}b \geq -18$ _____

Linear Equations & Inequalities 25

Solve.

a. $3(m - 1) - 4 \leq 2 - 4(2 - m)$ _____

b. $-3 + 2r \neq 9 - 2r$ _____

c. $\frac{2}{3}b < -8$ _____   d. $-2.5x \leq 12.5$ _____

Polynomials

Polynomials 1

Simplify.

a. 3^3 _____

b. 8^0 _____

c. $(-2)^{-2}$ _____

d. $8^6 \div 8^4$ _____

Polynomials 2

Rewrite each number in scientific notation.

a. 645

_____

b. 0.0023

_____

c. 48726.5

_____

d. $(3 \cdot 10^4)(4 \cdot 10^5)$

_____

Polynomials 3

Simplify. Assume that no variable equals 0.

a. $\dfrac{d^7}{d^4}$ _____

b. $\dfrac{c^2}{c^5}$ _____

c. $\dfrac{2ab^7}{5a^4}$ _____

d. $\dfrac{4x^2y^5}{2x^6y^2}$ _____

Polynomials 4

Simplify. Assume that no variable equals 0.

a. $(w^5)^6$ _____

b. $\left(\dfrac{-r}{s^3}\right)^8$ _____

c. $\left(\dfrac{4x}{5y}\right)^2$ _____

d. $\left(\dfrac{4u^2v}{-3u^5v^2}\right)^2$ _____

Polynomials

Polynomials 5

Simplify.

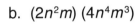

a. $(b^6)(b^3)$

_____

b. $(2n^2m)(4n^4m^3)$

_____

c. $(6x^3y)(3x^4y^4)$

_____

d. $(3a^{2x})(a^{3x})$

_____

Polynomials 6

State the degree in each polynomial.

a. $3n$

_____

b. $4x^2 - 2x + 6$

_____

c. $-10ab^3c^5$

_____

d. $5u^2v^2 + 8u^2v^2 + 3uv - 2$

_____

Polynomials 7

Write each monomial in factored form.

a. $-2b^3$

_____

b. $3^2x^5y^2$

_____

c. $-4a^2b^3$

_____

d. $(-x)^4$

_____

Polynomials 8

Rewrite each polynomial in descending order of the exponents with respect to x.

a. $2x - 5x^3 + 7 - x^4$

_____

b. $4x^3y^2 - x^8 + 2 - 3x^6y$

_____

c. $-6 + 8x^3y^4 - 3x^2y - 2x^5y^5$

_____

Polynomials

Polynomials 9

Solve.

a. $(3x^2 - 4x + 6) + (2x - 2x^2 + 2)$ _____

b. $(2m^3 - 4m^2 + m - 6) + (2m^2 + 6m^3 + 9)$ _____

Polynomials 10

Add these polynomials.

a. $(3x^3 + 2x^2 - 4x - 8) + (x^2 - 3x + 9)$

_____

b. $(3a^2 - 6a - 4) + (a^2 + 9 - 7a^3 + 2a)$

_____

Polynomials 11

Subtract.

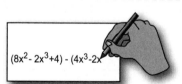
$(8x^2 - 2x^3 + 4) - (4x^3 - 2x$

a. $(7e^3 - 3e^2 + 9e + 1) - (3e^3 - e^2 + 5e - 7)$

_____

b. $(6b^3 + 3b^2 - b - 6) - (b^2 - 8b + 9)$

_____

Polynomials

Polynomials 12

Subtract.

a. $(r - 3r^2 + r^3 - 7) - (2r^3 - 4r + 6)$

_____

b. $(2y^4 + y^2 - y) - (y^2 + 2y)$

_____

Polynomials 13

If n is an integer, write an algebraic expression to find the sum of n and the next four consecutive integers. Then simplify.

_____

_____

Polynomials 14

Multiply.

a. $(-4b^4)(5b^5)$

_____

b. $3x^2y(4x + 2y - r)$

_____

c. $7m^2(m^3 - 3m^4 + 5m^2)$

_____

Polynomials 15

Multiply.

a. $(x + 5)(x - 8)$

_____

b. $(3a - 2)(5 + 6a)$

_____

c. $(2p - 3r)(4p + r)$

_____

Polynomials

Polynomials 16

Multiply.

a. $(2n - 3m)^2$

_____

b. $(y^2 + 2y + 1)(y - 5)$

_____

c. $(d - 2)(d - 2)(d - 2)$

_____

Polynomials 17

Multiply.

a. $(g + 5)(g - 5)$

_____

b. $(2a - b)^2$

_____

c. $(4h^5 + 3i^4)(4h^5 - 3i^4)$

_____

Polynomials 18

Divide.

a. $(16r^2 - 8r + 12) \div 4$

_____

b. $(12a^4 - 6a^2 + 4a) \div 2a$

_____

c. $(20n^5 + 10n^3 - 15n^2 + 5n) \div 5n$

_____

Polynomials 19

Divide.

a. $(2c^2 - 3c - 2) \div (c - 2)$

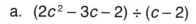

b. $(2y^2 + 3y - 20) \div (y + 4)$

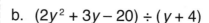

c. $(6x^2 - x - 12) \div (2x - 3)$

_____

Factoring

Factoring 1

Write each as the product of its factors by using exponents.

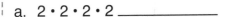

a. $2 \cdot 2 \cdot 2 \cdot 2$ _____

b. $3 \cdot 3 \cdot 5 \cdot 5 \cdot 5$ _____

c. $2 \cdot 5 \cdot 3 \cdot 3 \cdot 3$ _____

d. $11 \cdot 11 \cdot 11 \cdot 11 \cdot 11 \cdot 13 \cdot 13$

_____

Factoring 2

Write the prime factorization of each number. (Use exponents for repeated factors.)

a. 70 _____

b. 135 _____

c. 338 _____

d. 1,000 _____

Factoring 3

Factor.

a. $2m^3n - 12m^2n^4$

_____

b. $5x^2y - 15x^3y^3$

_____

c. $4g^2h + 8g^2h^2 + 12gh$

_____

Factoring 4

Factor.

a. $9a^2b^4 - 54a^5b^3$

_____

b. $2x^3 - 6x^2 + 10x$

_____

c. $-15c^3d^4 - 35c^4d^5 - 55c^2d^4$

_____

Factoring

Factoring 5

Factor.

a. $3p + 15$ _____

b. $2r + 7r^2$ _____

c. $16x + 12y$ _____

d. $4b^2 - 8b$ _____

Factoring 6

Factor.

a. $x^2 + 12x + 11$ _____

b. $48 + 19c + c^2$ _____

c. $m^2 - 9m + 14$ _____

d. $b^2 - 18b + 32$ _____

Factoring 7

Factor.

a. $3a^2 - 22a - 16$ _____

b. $2b^2 + 7b + 5$ _____

c. $3x^2 + 17x + 20$ _____

d. $5y^2 - 13y - 6$ _____

Factoring

Factoring 8

Factor.

a. $y^2 + 4y + 3$

_____

b. $7 + 8j + j^2$

_____

c. $k^2 + 14k + 13$

_____

d. $s^2 - 12s + 35$

_____

Factoring 9

Factor.

a. $x^2 - 16xy + 48y^2$

_____

b. $r^2 - 27rs + 72s^2$

_____

c. $u^4 - 16u^2 + 28$

_____

d. $a^2 + 32ab + 60b^2$

_____

Factoring 10

Factor.

a. $y^2 - y - 12$

_____

b. $x^2 + 6x - 7$

_____

c. $b^2 + 2b - 3$

_____

d. $r^2 - 13r - 30$

_____

Factoring 11

Factor.

a. $a^2 - ab - 2b^2$

_____

b. $m^2 - 14mn - 32n^2$

_____

c. $x^2 - 8xy - 20y^2$

_____

d. $r^4 - 23r^2 - 50$

_____

Factoring

Factoring 12

Factor.

a. $m^2 - 12m + 36$

_____

b. $t^2 + 20t + 100$

_____

c. $x^2 + 8x + 16$

_____

d. $r^2 + 26r + 169$

_____

Factoring 13

Factor.

a. $25a^2 + 10a + 1$

_____

b. $49c^2 + 14c + 1$

_____

c. $mn^3 - m^3n$

_____

d. $9h^{12} + 6h^6 + 1$

_____

Factoring 14

Factor by grouping.

a. $15x^2 + 12x + 6x^3$

_____

b. $5(y - 3) + 2(y - 3) - 3(y - 3)$

_____

c. $21a - 21b + 15a - 15b$

_____

d. $mr + nr + ms + ns$

_____

Factoring 15

Factor.

a. $y^2 - 5x - 25 + xy$

_____

b. $ab + ac - 3b - 3c$

_____

c. $mp - 2m + 3np - 6n$

_____

d. $2pq - 5qr - 4p + 10r$

_____

Factoring

Factoring 16

Solve by factoring.

a. $n^2 + 4n = 0$

_____

b. $3p^2 - 6p = 0$

_____

c. $5h^2 + 15h = 0$

_____

Factoring 17

Solve by factoring.

a. $x^2 - 6x + 9 = 0$

_____

b. $10a^3 - 29a^2 - 21a = 0$

_____

c. $y^5 - 10y^3 + 9y = 0$

_____

Factoring 18

Write an algebraic equation and solve it to find two consecutive integers whose product is 56.

_____

Factoring 19

Solve by factoring.

a. $2b(b - 3) = 0$

_____

b. $(2c - 6)(c + 6) = 0$

_____

c. $(4y - 3)(y + 5) = 0$

_____

Rational Expressions

Rational Expressions 1

State the value(s) of the variable for which each expression is undefined.

a. $\dfrac{3}{m-2}$ _____

b. $\dfrac{2r}{(r-5)(3r-2)}$ _____

c. $\dfrac{a+b}{2x+1}$ _____

d. $\dfrac{c-4}{c^2-16}$ _____

Rational Expressions 2

Simplify and state the values for which the expression is undefined.

a. $\dfrac{3a}{12a^2}$ _____

b. $\dfrac{7x-14}{x-2}$ _____

c. $\dfrac{r+2}{5r^2+7r-6}$ _____

d. $\dfrac{24y+18}{36}$ _____

Rational Expressions 3

Simplify and state the values for which the expression is undefined.

a. $\dfrac{2y^2+9y-5}{y^2+10y+25}$ _____

b. $\dfrac{9+11z+2z^2}{z^2-10z-11}$ _____

Rational Expressions 4

Multiply. Assume all denominators do not equal 0.

a. $\dfrac{5s}{3s^2} \cdot \dfrac{4}{s^2y}$ _____

b. $\dfrac{12xy^2}{5y^3z^2} \cdot \dfrac{5xz}{3x}$ _____

c. $\dfrac{2n+4}{3n-9} \cdot \dfrac{6n-18}{4n+20}$

_____

Rational Expressions

Rational Expressions 5

Multiply. Assume all denominators do not equal 0.

a. $\dfrac{h-5}{4h+6} \cdot \dfrac{6h+9}{3h-15}$ _____

b. $\dfrac{2y+4}{6y-8} \cdot \dfrac{y-5}{y+2}$ _____

c. $\dfrac{3b-15}{4b-2} \cdot \dfrac{20b-10}{15b-75}$ _____

Rational Expressions 6

Multiply. Assume all denominators do not equal 0.

a. $\dfrac{3m^2-10m-8}{2m} \cdot \dfrac{-2m-8}{m^2-16}$

_____

b. $\dfrac{b^2-3b-10}{(b-2)^2} \cdot \dfrac{b-2}{b-5}$

_____

Rational Expressions 7

Divide.

a. $\dfrac{2}{x} \div \dfrac{3y}{2x}$ _____

b. $\dfrac{a}{b} \div \dfrac{b^2}{a^3}$ _____

c. $\dfrac{9}{n} \div \dfrac{3r}{4n}$ _____

Rational Expressions 8

Divide.

a. $\dfrac{2x^2}{y^2} \div \dfrac{14x}{3y}$ _____

b. $\dfrac{c+5}{c+14} \div (c+5)$ _____

c. $\dfrac{s^2-9}{s^2-2s-24} \div \dfrac{s-3}{s-6}$ _____

Rational Expressions

Rational Expressions 9

Divide.

a. $\dfrac{5e^2 + 10e - 15}{e^2 - 6x + 5} \div \dfrac{2e^2 + 7e + 3}{4e^2 - 8e - 5}$

_____

b. $\dfrac{a^2 - a - 20}{a^2 + 7a + 12} \div \dfrac{a^2 - 10a + 25}{a^2 + 6a + 9}$

_____

Rational Expressions 10

Find the least common denominator.

a. $\dfrac{-3}{2a^3b}$ and $\dfrac{4a}{6a^3b^5}$

_____

b. $\dfrac{5}{12x^3y}$ and $\dfrac{-3}{10xy^2}$

_____

Rational Expressions 11

Find the least common denominator.

a. $\dfrac{1}{5mn}$ and $\dfrac{3n}{2m}$

_____

b. $\dfrac{7}{d^2 - 4}$ and $\dfrac{3}{d - 2}$

_____

Rational Expressions 12

Find the least common denominator and write the equivalent expressions with the LCD as denominator.

$$\dfrac{5}{9x^2y} \text{ and } \dfrac{2x}{3y^2}$$

a. LCD _____

b. Equivalent expressions

_____

Rational Expressions

Rational Expressions 13

Add or subtract.

a. $\dfrac{9}{2b} + \dfrac{3}{2b}$ _____

b. $\dfrac{2p}{p+1} + \dfrac{5p}{p+1}$ _____

c. $\dfrac{5x}{x+2} - \dfrac{x-8}{x+2}$ _____

Rational Expressions 14

Add or subtract.

a. $\dfrac{5b+1}{25-b^2} + \dfrac{5}{b+5}$ _____

b. $\dfrac{3}{2c} + \dfrac{2}{4c^2} - \dfrac{1}{c}$ _____

c. $\dfrac{4}{2y+8} - \dfrac{y}{5y+20}$ _____

Rational Expressions 15

Add or subtract.

a. $\dfrac{2}{4r^2} - \dfrac{2r+3}{6r^3}$ _____

b. $\dfrac{m}{m+2} + \dfrac{5}{m-6}$ _____

c. $\dfrac{5u-2}{u^2+u-20} - \dfrac{3}{u+5} + \dfrac{u}{u-4}$

_____

Rational Expressions 16

Simplify.

a. $2 + \dfrac{1}{e}$ _____

b. $5 - \dfrac{7}{y}$ _____

c. $3i - \dfrac{i+1}{i}$ _____

Rational Expressions

Rational Expressions 17

Simplify.

a. $\dfrac{2a-1}{a+2} + a$ _____

b. $\dfrac{\dfrac{k}{2} - \dfrac{k}{3}}{\dfrac{k}{6} + \dfrac{2}{3}}$ _____

Rational Expressions 18

Are these ratios equal?

a. $\dfrac{2}{5} = \dfrac{6}{15}$ _____

b. $\dfrac{4}{8} = \dfrac{9}{15}$ _____

c. $4:5 = 8:15$ _____

d. $2:8 = 12:48$ _____

Rational Expressions 19

Solve these ratios.

a. $\dfrac{5}{6} = \dfrac{30}{y}$ _____

b. $\dfrac{12d}{28} = \dfrac{15}{7}$ _____

c. $\dfrac{4}{24} = \dfrac{2}{6a}$ _____

Rational Expressions 20

A bag contains 10 red marbles, 4 green marbles, and 9 blue marbles. If you reached into the bag and took out 1 marble, what is the probability that ...

a. it will be red? _____

b. it will not be red? _____

c. it will be blue or red? _____

Linear Equations & Inequalities in Two Variables

Linear Equations & Inequalities in Two Variables 1

Name the point that is the graph of each ordered pair.

a. (-3, -4) _____

b. (2, -3) _____

c. (2, 2) _____

d. (-1, 1) _____

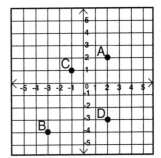

Linear Equations & Inequalities in Two Variables 2

Graph the ordered pairs and connect the points.

a. (1, 0)

b. (3, 2)

c. (-2, 3)

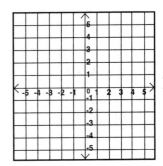

Linear Equations & Inequalities in Two Variables 3

Make a solution table for the equation.
Then graph the equation $y = 9 - 3x$.

x	y

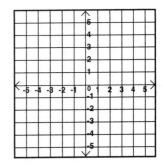

Linear Equations & Inequalities in Two Variables

Linear Equations & Inequalities in Two Variables 4

Determine if each ordered pair is a solution of the equation $x + 3y = 6$.

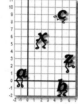

a. (3, 1) _____

b. (4, 2) _____

c. (9, -1) _____

d. (0, 2) _____

e. (-2, 2) _____

Linear Equations & Inequalities in Two Variables 5

Determine the missing coordinate of each ordered pair solution of $y = x + 6$.

a. (0, y) _____

b. (2, y) _____

c. (x, 0) _____

d. (x, 4) _____

Linear Equations & Inequalities in Two Variables 6

Find the x- and the y-intercepts of the graph of each equation.

	x-intercept	y-intercept
a. $x + y = 7$	_____	_____
b. $2x + y = 8$	_____	_____
c. $3x - y = 6$	_____	_____

Linear Equations & Inequalities in Two Variables 7

Graph the equation $x - y = 5$ using at least three points.

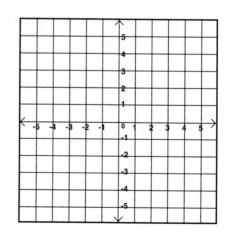

Linear Equations & Inequalities in Two Variables

Linear Equations & Inequalities in Two Variables 8

Graph the equation $2x + 2y = 8$ using at least three points.

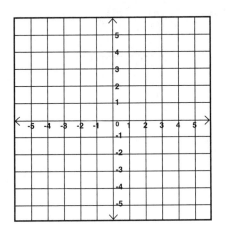

Linear Equations & Inequalities in Two Variables 9

Graph the equation $4y - x = 2$ using at least three points.

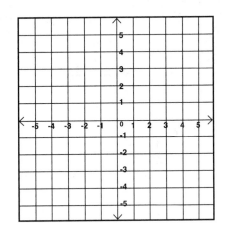

Linear Equations & Inequalities in Two Variables 10

Solve each equation for y.

a. $x + y = 8$

_____

b. $4x = 2y - 1$

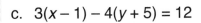

_____

c. $3(x - 1) - 4(y + 5) = 12$

_____

Linear Equations & Inequalities in Two Variables 11

Find the slope of a line that contains the given points.

a. A (-2, 3) B (2, 1) _____

b. C (6, 7) D (1, 3) _____

c. E (-1, 3) F (2, 4) _____

Linear Equations & Inequalities in Two Variables

Linear Equations & Inequalities in Two Variables 12

Find the slope of a line that contains the given points.

a. A (1, 3) B (2, 3) _____

b. C (5, -2) D (4, 3) _____

c. E (3, 8) F (1, 4) _____

Linear Equations & Inequalities in Two Variables 13

Find the value of the missing coordinate using the given slope.

A (x, 0) and B (3, 4), slope = 2

_____

Linear Equations & Inequalities in Two Variables 14

Find the slope and the y-intercept of the line for the given equation.

$$4x + 3y = 12$$

slope _____

y-intercept _____

Linear Equations & Inequalities in Two Variables 15

Find the slope and the y-intercept of the line for the given equation.

$$8x - y = 2$$

slope _____

y-intercept _____

Linear Equations & Inequalities in Two Variables

Linear Equations & Inequalities in Two Variables 16

Write an equation in slope-intercept form that contains the given points.

A (5, 6) B (6, 9)

_____

Linear Equations & Inequalities in Two Variables 17

Write an equation of a line in standard form given a point and the slope.

point (0, 3)   slope: $-\frac{1}{2}$

_____

Linear Equations & Inequalities in Two Variables 18

Graph the inequality $x \geq 2$.

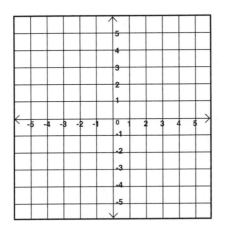

Linear Equations & Inequalities in Two Variables 19

Graph the inequality $y \geq -x + 3$.

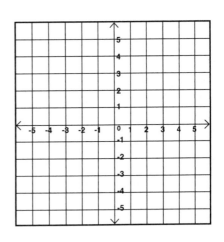

Systems of Linear Equations & Inequalities

Systems of Linear Equations & Inequalities 1

Solve by graphing:

$$\left\{ \begin{array}{c} x - 2y = 1 \\ x + 2y = 1 \end{array} \right\}$$

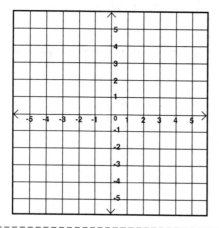

Systems of Linear Equations & Inequalities 2

Without graphing, describe the graph and tell the number of solutions.

$$\left\{ \begin{array}{c} 8x - 6y = 2 \\ 6x - 8y = 2 \end{array} \right\}$$

_____

_____

_____

_____

Systems of Linear Equations & Inequalities 3

Solve by substitution.

a. $\left\{ \begin{array}{c} y = 2x \\ 7x - y = 35 \end{array} \right\}$

_____

b. $\left\{ \begin{array}{c} 3x - y = 17 \\ y + 2x = 8 \end{array} \right\}$

_____

Systems of Linear Equations & Inequalities 4

Solve by substitution.

a. $\left\{ \begin{array}{c} 3x + 2y = 4 \\ y = x - 3 \end{array} \right\}$

_____

b. $\left\{ \begin{array}{c} y = 3x + 1 \\ y = 6x - 1 \end{array} \right\}$

_____

Systems of Linear Equations & Inequalities

Systems of Linear Equations & Inequalities 5

Solve by substitution.

a. $\left\{ \begin{array}{l} x - y = 0 \\ x + y = 2 \end{array} \right\}$

_____

b. $\left\{ \begin{array}{l} 3x + 2y = 9 \\ x + y = 3 \end{array} \right\}$

_____

Systems of Linear Equations & Inequalities 6

Solve by elimination.

a. $\left\{ \begin{array}{l} x + y = 10 \\ x - y = 12 \end{array} \right\}$

_____

b. $\left\{ \begin{array}{l} -x + y = 4 \\ x + y = 8 \end{array} \right\}$

_____

Systems of Linear Equations & Inequalities 7

Solve by elimination.

a. $\left\{ \begin{array}{l} x + y = 0 \\ x - y = -6 \end{array} \right\}$

_____

b. $\left\{ \begin{array}{l} 7x + y = 22 \\ 5x - y = 14 \end{array} \right\}$

_____

Systems of Linear Equations & Inequalities 8

Solve by elimination.

a. $\left\{ \begin{array}{l} 2x = y + 1 \\ 2y - x = 1 \end{array} \right\}$

_____

b. $\left\{ \begin{array}{l} 2x - 5y = 17 \\ 6x = 5y + 1 \end{array} \right\}$

_____

Systems of Linear Equations & Inequalities

Systems of Linear Equations & Inequalities 9

Write an equation for each word sentence.

a. A number *n* is four more than two times a number *m*.

   _____

b. A number *a* is half as much as three less than a number *b*.

   _____

Systems of Linear Equations & Inequalities 10

Write an equation for each word sentence.

a. Six years from now, Steve will be 4 years older than twice

   Roy's age now. _____

b. The amount of money in dimes is half the amount of money

   in quarters. _____

Systems of Linear Equations & Inequalities 11

Write a system of linear equations for the problem and then solve.

The sum of two numbers is 36. If the smaller number is subtracted from the larger number, the difference is 4.

   _____

Systems of Linear Equations & Inequalities

Systems of Linear Equations & Inequalities 12

Write a system of linear equations for the problem and then solve.

Pam has 26 coins in nickels and quarters. Together they are worth $3.10. How many of each coin does she have?

_____

_____

Systems of Linear Equations & Inequalities 13

Write a system of linear equations for the problem and then solve.

Together José and Dan sold 137 candy bars for the fundraiser. If José sold 10 fewer than twice as many as Dan, how many did each of them sell?

_____

_____

Systems of Linear Equations & Inequalities 14

Write a system of linear equations for the problem and then solve.

Ella is 3 years older than Marta. Four years ago, Ella was twice as old as Marta. How old are they both now?

_____

_____

Systems of Linear Equations & Inequalities 15

Write a system of linear equations for the problem and then solve.

David is 3 times as old as Alex. In three years, the sum of their ages will be 54. How old is each of them now?

_____

_____

Square Roots & Radicals

Square Roots & Radicals 1

Find the square roots.

a. $\sqrt{49}$ _____

b. $\pm\sqrt{0.81}$ _____

c. $-\sqrt{\dfrac{1}{16}}$ _____

d. $\sqrt{900}$ _____

Square Roots & Radicals 2

Find the square roots.

a. $\pm\sqrt{576}$ _____

b. $\sqrt{0.0025}$ _____

c. $-\sqrt{-(2-11)}$ _____

d. $-\sqrt{1.96}$ _____

Square Roots & Radicals 3

Simplify.

a. $\sqrt[4]{81}$ _____

b. $\sqrt[5]{32}$ _____

c. $\sqrt[3]{64}$ _____

d. $\sqrt[3]{-125}$ _____

Square Roots & Radicals 4

Simplify.

a. $\sqrt{72}$ _____

b. $\sqrt{108}$ _____

c. $\sqrt{44}$ _____

d. $\sqrt{90}$ _____

Square Roots & Radicals

Square Roots & Radicals 5

Simplify.

a. $\sqrt{24}$ _____

b. $\sqrt{150}$ _____

c. $\sqrt{48}$ _____

d. $\sqrt{1,000}$ _____

Square Roots & Radicals 6

Evaluate for the given value of the variable and then simplify, if possible.

a. $\sqrt{a-7}$, $a = 15$ _____

b. $\sqrt{b+3}$, $b = 25$ _____

c. $\sqrt{3c+6}$, $c = 7$ _____

Square Roots & Radicals 7

Simplify. Assume all variables represent non-negative real numbers.

a. $\sqrt{9a^3b^4}$ _____

b. $\sqrt{\frac{50}{49}}$ _____

c. $\dfrac{9}{\sqrt{5}}$ _____

d. $\sqrt{\frac{25}{81}}$ _____

Square Roots & Radicals 8

Simplify. Assume all variables represent non-negative real numbers.

a. $4\sqrt{11} + 3\sqrt{11}$ _____

b. $8\sqrt{15} - 4\sqrt{15}$ _____

c. $\sqrt{6} - 4\sqrt{6}$ _____

Square Roots & Radicals

Square Roots & Radicals 9

Simplify. Assume all variables represent non-negative real numbers.

a. $-5\sqrt{x} + \sqrt{9x}$ _____

b. $\sqrt{16r} - \sqrt{r}$ _____

c. $4\sqrt{12} + 5\sqrt{27}$ _____

Square Roots & Radicals 10

Simplify.

a. $\sqrt{x^4 y}$ _____

b. $\sqrt{81y^9}$ _____

c. $\sqrt{b^4 c^6}$ _____

d. $\sqrt{88r^4}$ _____

Square Roots & Radicals 11

Simplify. Assume variables represent non-negative real numbers.

a. $11\sqrt{5} - 2\sqrt{20} + 4\sqrt{45}$

_____

b. $\sqrt{9n} - \sqrt{16n} + \sqrt{25n}$

_____

Square Roots & Radicals 12

Simplify. Assume variables represent non-negative real numbers.

a. $3\sqrt{36y} + \sqrt{100y} - 2\sqrt{64y}$

_____

b. $\sqrt{b} - 7\sqrt{b} + 6\sqrt{b}$

_____

Square Roots & Radicals

Square Roots & Radicals 13

Multiply and simplify.

a. $(\sqrt{5})(\sqrt{10})$ _____

b. $(2\sqrt{3})(-3\sqrt{2})$ _____

c. $(\sqrt{\frac{9}{2}})(\sqrt{\frac{2}{3}})$ _____

Square Roots & Radicals 14

Multiply and simplify.

a. $(\sqrt{2} + 3)(\sqrt{2} - 3)$ _____

b. $\sqrt{7}(4 + \sqrt{7})$ _____

c. $(4\sqrt{n})^2$ _____

Square Roots & Radicals 15

Rationalize the denominator and simplify.

a. $\sqrt{\frac{1}{2}}$
b. $\frac{-2\sqrt{3}}{\sqrt{5}}$
c. $\frac{3\sqrt{2}}{4\sqrt{32}}$

_____ _____ _____

Square Roots & Radicals

Square Roots & Radicals 16

Rationalize the denominator and simplify.

a. $\dfrac{4\sqrt{3}}{2\sqrt{8}}$

b. $\sqrt{\dfrac{8}{y}}$

c. $\sqrt{\dfrac{24x^3}{6x}}$

_____   _____   _____

Square Roots & Radicals 17

Solve these radical equations.

a. $\sqrt{g} = 8$

b. $\sqrt{\dfrac{b}{3}} = 2$

c. $\sqrt{2y-1} - 3 = 1$

_____   _____   _____

Square Roots & Radicals 18

Solve these radical equations.

a. $\sqrt{s-2} = 3$

b. $\sqrt{\dfrac{2n}{3}} + 5 = 7$

c. $5\sqrt{x} = 10$

_____   _____   _____

Square Roots & Radicals

Square Roots & Radicals 19

Use the Pythagorean Theorem ($a^2 + b^2 = c^2$) to find the missing lengths.

a. $a = 5$, $c = 13$, $b = ?$ _____

b. $b = 4$, $c = 5$, $a = ?$ _____

c. $a = \sqrt{3}$, $b = 1$, $c = ?$ _____

Square Roots & Radicals 20

Use the Pythagorean Theorem ($a^2 + b^2 = c^2$) to find the distance between each pair of points.

a. R (1, 2), S (4, -2)

b. B (6, 2), C (6, -8)

Quadratic Equations

Quadratic Equations 1

Solve by factoring. Express all radicals in simplest form.

a. $u^2 - u - 12 = 0$ _____

b. $4a^2 - 9a = 0$ _____

c. $6b^2 = 17b - 12$ _____

Quadratic Equations 2

Solve by factoring. Express all radicals in simplest form.

a. $3d^2 - 10 = 13d$ _____

b. $7c^2 - 12c = 0$ _____

c. $5x^2 + 13x = 6$ _____

Quadratic Equations 3

Solve by the square-root method. Express all radicals in simplest form.

a. $r^2 = \sqrt{\dfrac{4}{25}}$ _____

b. $36b^2 = 18$ _____

c. $2r^2 = 16$ _____

Quadratic Equations

Quadratic Equations 4

Solve by the square-root method. Express all radicals in simplest form.

a. $g^2 - 49 = 0$ _____

b. $h^2 - 169 = 0$ _____

c. $25x^2 - 81 = 0$ _____

Quadratic Equations 5

Solve by the square-root method. Express all radicals in simplest form.

a. $(b - 1)^2 = 9$ _____

b. $3g^2 - 36 = 0$ _____

c. $(7e + 3)^2 = 16$ _____

Quadratic Equations 6

Solve by completing the square. Express all radicals in simplest form.

$b^2 + 5b + 6 = 0$

a. $a^2 - 2a - 8 = 0$ _____

b. $c^2 + 10c + 3 = 0$ _____

c. $4r^2 - 12r = -9$ _____

Quadratic Equations

Quadratic Equations 7

Solve by completing the square. Express all radicals in simplest form.

a. $2x^2 - 2x - 2 = 0$

_____

b. $b^2 + 12b = 45$

_____

c. $a^2 - 4a + 2 = 0$

_____

Quadratic Equations 8

Solve by using the quadratic formula.

a. $2a^2 - 3a - 5 = 0$

_____

b. $b^2 + 5b + 6 = 0$

_____

Quadratic Equations 9

Solve by using the quadratic formula.

a. $x^2 - 3x - 10 = 0$

_____

b. $r^2 - 3r + 6 = 4$

_____

Quadratic Equations 10

Solve each quadratic equation by any appropriate method.

a. $4y^2 - 20 = 0$

_____

b. $s^2 - 4s = -3$

_____

Quadratic Equations

Quadratic Equations 11

Solve by factoring. Express all radicals in simplest form.

a. $x^2 - 7x = 0$

_____

b. $2x^2 - 9x = 0$

_____

c. $x^2 + 6x + 8 = 0$

_____

Quadratic Equations 12

Solve by completing the square. Express all radicals in simplest form.

a. $x^2 - 3x + 2 = 0$

_____

b. $x^2 - 16x + 60 = 0$

_____

Quadratic Equations 13

Solve by using the quadratic formula.

a. $2x^2 + 3x - 5 = 0$

_____

b. $c^2 - 11c + 28 = 0$

_____

Quadratic Equations 14

Solve by using the quadratic formula.

a. $5m^2 = m + 4$

_____

b. $7y + 6 = 3y^2$

_____

Student Reference Page

Order of Operations

Always solve equations in this order:
1. Perform operations inside parentheses.
2. Simplify exponents.
3. Multiply and divide from left to right.
4. Add and subtract from left to right.

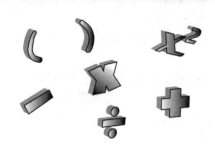

Property of Equality

If you add, subtract, multiply, or divide both sides of a true equation by the same amount, the equation remains true.

Commutative Property of Addition

The sum of two or more numbers always remains the same, no matter the order in which they are added. *Examples:* 2 + 3 + 4 + 5 = 14 and 5 + 4 + 3 + 2 = 14

Commutative Property of Multiplication

The product of two or more numbers always remains the same, no matter the order in which they are multiplied. *Examples:* 2 x 3 x 4 = 24 and 4 x 2 x 3 = 24

Multiplication of Positive and Negative Numbers

When multiplying two or more positive numbers, the answer will always be a positive number. *Example:* 2 x 3 x 4 = 24

When multiplying a positive number by a negative number, the answer will always be a negative number. *Example:* -5 x 4 = -20

When multiplying a negative number by a negative number, the answer will always be a positive number. *Example:* -5 x -4 = 20

Division of Positive and Negative Numbers

When dividing a positive number by a positive number, the answer will always be a positive number. *Example:* 49 ÷ 7 = 7

When dividing a negative number by a negative number, the answer will always be a positive number. *Example:* -49 ÷ -7 = 7

When dividing a negative number by a positive number, the answer will always be a negative number. *Example:* -49 ÷ 7 = -7

When dividing a positive number by a negative number, the answer will always be a negative number. *Example:* 49 ÷ -7 = -7

Answer Keys

Real Numbers 1 (p. 2)
A = 1; B = 1.5; C = -3; D = 2

Real Numbers 2 (p. 2)

Real Numbers 3 (p. 2)
a. <   b. >   c. =   d. >

Real Numbers 4 (p. 3)

a. $(-2, -\frac{3}{4}, 0, 1\frac{1}{3}, 4)$
b. $(-3, -2.8, 4.10, 4.6, \sqrt{25})$

Real Numbers 5 (p. 3)

a. 4   b. $\frac{1}{5}$ c. 16   d. 9.1

Real Numbers 6 (p. 3)
a. -11   b. -50   c. 1
d. 20   e. 2

Real Numbers 7 (p. 3)
a. -20   b. 72   c. -9.03
d. $\frac{8}{15}$ e. -90

Real Numbers 8 (p. 4)
a. -27   b. -4   c. $\frac{3}{4}$
d. 0   e. -17.5

Real Numbers 9 (p. 4)
a. 3   b. -7   c. 133   d. -926
e. 2.9   f. $-\frac{2}{15}$

Real Numbers 10 (p. 4)
70°

Real Numbers 11 (p. 4)
a. T   b. F   c. T   d. F
e. T

Real Numbers 12 (p. 5)

a. $-\frac{1}{3}$ b. $\frac{1}{\sqrt{21}}$ c. $\frac{4}{3}$

d. $-\frac{1}{2}$ e. $\frac{8}{19}$ f. $\frac{\sqrt{7}}{12}$

Real Numbers 13 (p. 5)
2, 4, 1, 3

Real Numbers 14 (p. 5)
a. 8   b. 17   c. 48

Real Numbers 15 (p. 5)
a. 16   b. 39   c. 4

Algebraic Expressions 1 (p. 6)
a. 27   b. 38   c. 84   d. 3

Algebraic Expressions 2 (p. 6)
a. 90   b. 6.5   c. 25

Algebraic Expressions 3 (p. 6)

a. $\frac{3}{4}$ b. $\frac{1}{4}$ c. $\frac{1}{8}$ d. $\frac{1}{2}$

Algebraic Expressions 4 (p. 6)
a. $n - 3$ b. $n + 8$ c. $50 - n$

Algebraic Expressions 5 (p. 7)
a. $n + 8$ b. $12 - s$ c. $4t - 3$

d. $\frac{g}{h}$

Algebraic Expressions 6 (p. 7)
a. 12   b. 72   c. 13   d. -36

Algebraic Expressions 7 (p. 7)
a. 16   b. 27   c. -1   d. 12

Algebraic Expressions 8 (p. 7)
a. 0   b. 25   c. 36   d. -125

Algebraic Expressions 9 (p. 8)
a. 14   b. 7   c. 6   d. 14

Algebraic Expressions 10 (p. 8)
a. $\frac{1}{3}$ b. 50   c. 2

Algebraic Expressions 11 (p. 8)
a. unlike   b. unlike   c. like
d. like

Algebraic Expressions 12 (p. 8)
a. 6   b. 1   c. 5   d. 10
e. 18

Algebraic Expressions 13 (p. 9)
a. $6n + 8n^2$ b. $7x^2y - 3xy$
c. $9b - 18$ d. $6a^3b + 9ab^3$

Algebraic Expressions 14 (p. 9)
a. $2ab^2 - 7ab$ b. $6x - y$
c. $7g^3 - 3h - 32$

Algebraic Expressions 15 (p. 9)
a. $6n$ b. $-7y$ c. $2t + 11$
d. $8b^2$ e. $3x + 6$
f. $3x^3y + 4xy$

Algebraic Expressions 16 (p. 10)
a. $3n + 5$ b. $4(n + 6)$ c. $8n^2 - 2$

Algebraic Expressions 17 (p. 10)
a. $b = g + 4$ b. $g + 1 = 2b$

Algebraic Expressions 18 (p. 10)
a. $\{0\}$ b. $\{-1\}$ c. $\{-1, 0\}$ d. $\{\ \}$

Algebraic Expressions 19 (p. 10)
a. $5n + 35 = 110$ b. $25 + 2n = 105$

Linear Equations & Inequalities 1 (p. 11)
a. Subtract 3.   b. Add 1.
c. Add 6.   d. Subtract 12.

Linear Equations & Inequalities 2 (p. 11)
a. 28   b. 15   c. 11   d. -22

Linear Equations & Inequalities 3 (p. 11)
a. 6   b. -6.1   c. $2\frac{2}{3}$ d. 8.35

Linear Equations & Inequalities 4 (p. 11)
$n - 32 = 11, n = 43$

Linear Equations & Inequalities 5 (p. 12)
a. no   b. yes   c. yes

Linear Equations & Inequalities 6 (p. 12)
a. no   b. yes   c. yes

Linear Equations & Inequalities 7 (p. 12)
a. $A = 15$ b. $h = 8$ c. $b = 6$

Linear Equations & Inequalities 8 (p. 13)
a. Divide by 6.   b. Multiply by $\frac{3}{2}$.
c. Divide by -3.

Linear Equations & Inequalities 9 (p. 13)
a. -6   b. 7   c. -28   d. 20

Linear Equations and Inequalities 10 (p. 13)

a. 4   b. 6   c. 50   d. -4

Linear Equations & Inequalities 11 (p. 13)

a. $\dfrac{30}{n} = 6, n = 5$ b. $9c = 27, c = 3$

Linear Equations & Inequalities 12 (p. 14)

a. 3   b. 5   c. -7   d. 9

Linear Equations & Inequalities 13 (p. 14)

a. 8   b. 80   c. 7   d. 12

Linear Equations & Inequalities 14 (p. 14)

a. 9   b. 7   c. 30   d. 11

Linear Equations & Inequalities 15 (p. 14)

a. $3x - 10 = 50, x = 20$
b. $n + 5n = 12, n = 2$

Linear Equations & Inequalities 16 (p. 15)

a. $C = 62.8$ b. $r = 15$

Linear Equations & Inequalities 17 (p. 15)

a. $6n - 24$ b. $15 + 3d$
c. $100 + 75s$ d. $3a + 3b$

Linear Equations & Inequalities 18 (p. 15)

a. 3   b. 9   c. 2   d. 2.5

Linear Equations & Inequalities 19 (p. 15)

a. 7.84   b. 25%   c. 150   d. 7.75

Linear Equations & Inequalities 20 (p. 16)

a. 1   b. -2   c. 3   d. 2

Linear Equations & Inequalities 21 (p. 16)

a. $\{1, -8\}$ b. $\{18, -6\}$
c. $y > 10, y < -2$ d. $g \le 4, g \ge 5$

Linear Equations & Inequalities 22 (p. 16)

a

Linear Equations & Inequalities 23 (p. 17)

a. -1   b. $\frac{6}{7}$ c. -3

Linear Equations & Inequalities 24 (p. 17)

a. $y < -6$ b. $x \ge 1$ c. $c < 7$
d. $b \ge -24$

Linear Equations & Inequalities 25 (p. 17)

a. $m \ge -1$ b. $r \ne 3$ c. $b < -12$
d. $x \ge -5$

Polynomials 1 (p. 18)

a. 27   b. 1   c. $\frac{1}{4}$ d. 64

Polynomials 2 (p. 18)

a. $6.45 \cdot 10^2$ b. $2.3 \cdot 10^{-3}$
c. $4.87265 \cdot 10^4$ d. $1.2 \cdot 10^{10}$

Polynomials 3 (p. 18)

a. d^3 b. $\dfrac{1}{c^3}$ c. $\dfrac{2b^7}{5a^3}$ d. $\dfrac{2y^3}{x^4}$

Polynomials 4 (p. 18)

a. w^{30} b. $\dfrac{r^8}{s^{24}}$ c. $\dfrac{16x^2}{25y^2}$ d. $\dfrac{16}{9u^6v^2}$

Polynomials 5 (p. 19)

a. b^9 b. $8n^6m^4$ c. $18x^7y^5$

d. $3a^{5x}$

Polynomials 6 (p. 19)

a. 1   b. 2   c. 9   d. 4

Polynomials 7 (p. 19)

a. $-2 \cdot b \cdot b \cdot b$

b. $3 \cdot 3 \cdot x \cdot x \cdot x \cdot x \cdot x \cdot y \cdot y$

c. $-4 \cdot a \cdot a \cdot b \cdot b \cdot b$

d. $(-x)\,(-x)\,(-x)\,(-x)$

Polynomials 8 (p. 19)

a. $-x^4 - 5x^3 + 2x + 7$

b. $-x^8 - 3x^6y + 4x^3y^2 + 2$

c. $-2x^5y^5 + 8x^3y^4 - 3x^2y - 6$

Polynomials 9 (p. 20)

a. $x^2 - 2x + 8$

b. $8m^3 - 2m^2 + m + 3$

Polynomials 10 (p. 20)

a. $3x^3 + 3x^2 - 7x + 1$

b. $-7a^3 + 4a^2 - 4a + 5$

Polynomials 11 (p. 20)

a. $4e^3 - 2e^2 + 4e + 8$

b. $6b^3 + 2b^2 + 7b - 15$

Polynomials 12 (p. 21)

a. $-r^3 - 3r^2 + 5r - 13$

b. $2y^4 - 3y$

Polynomials 13 (p. 21)

$5n + 10$

Polynomials 14 (p. 21)

a. $-20b^9$ b. $12x^3y + 6x^2y^2 - 3x^2yr$

c. $7m^5 - 21m^6 + 35m^4$

Polynomials 15 (p. 21)

a. $x^2 - 3x - 40$ b. $18a^2 + 3a - 10$

c. $8p^2 - 10pr - 3r^2$

Polynomials 16 (p. 22)

a. $4n^2 - 12nm + 9m^2$

b. $y^3 - 3y^2 - 9y - 5$

c. $d^3 - 6d^2 + 12d - 8$

Polynomials 17 (p. 22)

a. $g^2 - 25$ b. $4a^2 - 4ab + b^2$

c. $16h^{10} - 9i^8$

Polynomials 18 (p. 22)

a. $4r^2 - 2r + 3$ b. $6a^3 - 3a + 2$

c. $4n^4 + 2n^2 - 3n + 1$

Polynomials 19 (p. 22)

a. $2c + 1$ b. $2y - 5$ c. $3x + 4$

Factoring 1 (p. 23)

a. 2^4 b. $3^2 \cdot 5^3$ c. $2 \cdot 5 \cdot 3^3$

d. $11^5 \cdot 13^2$

Factoring 2 (p. 23)

a. $2 \cdot 5 \cdot 7$ b. $3^3 \cdot 5$ c. $2 \cdot 13^2$

d. $2^3 \cdot 5^3$

Factoring 3 (p. 23)

a. $2m^2n(m - 6n^3)$

b. $5x^2y(1 - 3xy^2)$

c. $4gh(g + 2gh + 3)$

Factoring 4 (p. 23)

a. $9a^2b^3(b - 6a^3)$ b. $2x(x^2 - 3x + 5)$

c. $-5c^2d^4(3c + 7c^2d + 11)$

Factoring 5 (p. 24)

a. $3(p + 5)$ b. $r(2 + 7r)$
c. $4(4x + 3y)$ or $2(8x + 6y)$
d. $4b(b - 2)$ or $2b(2b - 4)$

Factoring 6 (p. 24)

a. $(x + 1)(x + 11)$ b. $(3 + c)(16 + c)$
c. $(m - 2)(m - 7)$ d. $(b - 2)(b - 16)$

Factoring 7 (p. 24)

a. $(3a + 2)(a - 8)$ b. $(2b + 5)(b + 1)$
c. $(3x + 5)(x + 4)$ d. $(5y + 2)(y - 3)$

Factoring 8 (p. 25)

a. $(y + 1)(y + 3)$ b. $(1 + j)(7 + j)$
c. $(k + 1)(k + 13)$ d. $(s - 5)(s - 7)$

Factoring 9 (p. 25)

a. $(x - 4y)(x - 12y)$
b. $(r - 3s)(r - 24s)$
c. $(u^2 - 2)(u^2 - 14)$
d. $(a + 2b)(a + 30b)$

Factoring 10 (p. 25)

a. $(y - 4)(y + 3)$ b. $(x + 7)(x - 1)$
c. $(b + 3)(b - 1)$ d. $(r - 15)(r + 2)$

Factoring 11 (p. 25)

a. $(a - 2b)(a + b)$
b. $(m - 16n)(m + 2n)$
c. $(x - 10y)(x + 2y)$
d. $(r^2 - 25)(r^2 + 2)$

Factoring 12 (p. 26)

a. $(m - 6)^2$ b. $(t + 10)^2$
c. $(x + 4)^2$ d. $(r + 13)^2$

Factoring 13 (p. 26)

a. $(5a + 1)^2$ b. $(7c + 1)^2$
c. $mn(n^2 - m^2)$ d. $(3h^6 + 1)^2$

Factoring 14 (p. 26)

a. $3x(5x + 4 + 2x^2)$ b. $4(y - 3)$
c. $36(a - b)$ d. $(m + n)(r + s)$

Factoring 15 (p. 26)

a. $(y - 5)(y + 5 + x)$
b. $(b + c)(a - 3)$
c. $(p - 2)(m + 3n)$
d. $(q - 2)(2p - 5r)$

Factoring 16 (p. 27)

a. $n = 0, -4$ b. $p = 0, 2$
c. $h = 0, -3$

Factoring 17 (p. 27)

a. $x = 3$ b. $a = 0, -\frac{3}{5}, \frac{7}{2}$
c. $y = 0, -3, 3, -1, 1$

Factoring 18 (p. 27)

$n(n + 1) = 56$; $n = 7$ or -8
The two integers are 7 and 8 or -7 and -8.

Factoring 19 (p. 27)

a. $b = 0, 3$ b. $c = 3, -6$
c. $y = \frac{3}{4}, -5$

Rational Expressions 1 (p. 28)

a. 2 b. $5, \frac{2}{3}$ c. $-\frac{1}{2}$
d. -4, 4

Rational Expressions 2 (p. 28)

a. $\frac{1}{4a}$, $a \neq 0$ b. $7, x \neq 2$

c. $\frac{1}{5r - 3}$, $r \neq \frac{3}{5}, -3$ d. $\frac{4y + 3}{6}$
There is no value where the expression is undefined.

Rational Expressions 3 (p. 28)

a. $\dfrac{2y-1}{y+5}$, $y \ne -5$

b. $\dfrac{2z+9}{z-11}$, $z \ne 11, -1$

Rational Expressions 4 (p. 28)

a. $\dfrac{20}{3s^3y}$ b. $\dfrac{4x}{yz}$ c. $\dfrac{n+2}{n+5}$

Rational Expressions 5 (p. 29)

a. $\frac{1}{2}$ b. $\dfrac{y-5}{3y-4}$ c. 1

Rational Expressions 6 (p. 29)

a. $-\dfrac{3m+2}{m}$ b. $\dfrac{b+2}{b-2}$

Rational Expressions 7 (p. 29)

a. $\dfrac{4}{3y}$ b. $\dfrac{a^4}{b^3}$ c. $\dfrac{12}{r}$

Rational Expressions 8 (p. 29)

a. $\dfrac{3x}{7y}$ b. $\dfrac{1}{c+14}$ c. $\dfrac{s+3}{s+4}$

Rational Expressions 9 (p. 30)

a. $\dfrac{5(2e-5)}{e-5}$ b. $\dfrac{a+3}{a-5}$

Rational Expressions 10 (p. 30)

a. $6a^3b^5$ b. $60x^3y^2$

Rational Expressions 11 (p. 30)

a. $10mn$ b. $(d+2)(d-2)$

Rational Expressions 12 (p. 30)

a. $9x^2y^2$ b. $\dfrac{5y}{9x^2y^2}$ $\dfrac{6x^3}{9x^2y^2}$

Rational Expressions 13 (p. 31)

a. $\dfrac{6}{b}$ b. $\dfrac{7p}{p+1}$ c. 4

Rational Expressions 14 (p. 31)

a. $\dfrac{26}{(5-b)(b+5)}$ b. $\dfrac{c+1}{2c^2}$

c. $\dfrac{10-y}{5(y+4)}$

Rational Expressions 15 (p. 31)

a. $\dfrac{r-3}{6r^3}$ b. $\dfrac{m^2-m+10}{(m+2)(m-6)}$

c. $\dfrac{u+2}{u-4}$

Rational Expressions 16 (p. 31)

a. $\dfrac{2e+1}{e}$ b. $\dfrac{5y-7}{y}$

c. $\dfrac{3i^2-i-1}{i}$

Rational Expressions 17 (p. 32)

a. $\dfrac{a^2+4a-1}{a+2}$ b. $\dfrac{k}{k+4}$

Rational Expressions 18 (p. 32)

a. yes   b. no   c. no   d. yes

Rational Expressions 19 (p. 32)

a. 36   b. 5   c. 2

Rational Expressions 20 (p. 32)

a. $\frac{10}{23}$ b. $\frac{13}{23}$ c. $\frac{19}{23}$

Linear Equations & Inequalities in Two Variables 1 (p. 33)

a. B   b. D

c. A   d. C

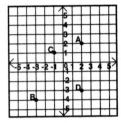

Linear Equations & Inequalities in Two Variables 2 (p. 33)

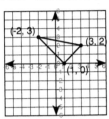

Linear Equations & Inequalities in Two Variables 3 (p. 33)

Table will vary.

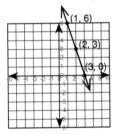

Linear Equations & Inequalities in Two Variables 4 (p. 34)

a. yes   b. no   c. yes   d. yes

e. no

Linear Equations & Inequalities in Two Variables 5 (p. 34)

a. 6   b. 8   c. -6   d. -2

Linear Equations and Inequalities in Two Variables 6 (p. 34)

	x-intercept	y-intercept
a.	7	7
b.	4	8
c.	2	-6

Linear Equations & Inequalities in Two Variables 7 (p. 34)

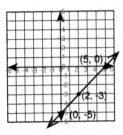

Linear Equations & Inequalities in Two Variables 8 (p. 35)

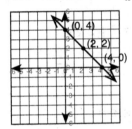

Linear Equations & Inequalities in Two Variables 9 (p. 35)

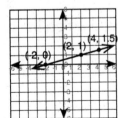

Linear Equations & Inequalities in Two Variables 10 (p. 35)

a. $y = 8 - x$ b. $y = \dfrac{4x + 1}{2}$

c. $y = \dfrac{3x - 35}{4}$

Linear Equations & Inequalities in Two Variables 11 (p. 35)

a. $-\frac{1}{2}$ b. $\frac{4}{5}$ c. $\frac{1}{3}$

Linear Equations & Inequalities in Two Variables 12 (p. 36)

a. 0   b. -5   c. 2

Linear Equations & Inequalities in Two Variables 13 (p. 36)

$x = 1$

Linear Equations & Inequalities in Two Variables 14 (p. 36)

slope $= -\frac{4}{3}$ y-intercept $= 4$

Linear Equations & Inequalities in Two Variables 15 (p. 36)

slope $= 8$ y-intercept $= -2$

Linear Equations & Inequalities in Two Variables 16 (p. 37)

$y = 3x - 9$

Linear Equations & Inequalities in Two Variables 17 (p. 37)

$x + 2y = 6$

Linear Equations & Inequalities in Two Variables 18 (p. 37)

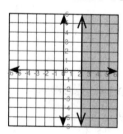

Linear Equations & Inequalities in Two Variables 19 (p. 37)

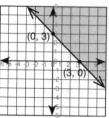

Systems of Linear Equations & Inequalities 1 (p. 38)

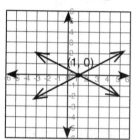

Systems of Linear Equations & Inequalities 2 (p. 38)

intersecting lines; one solution

Systems of Linear Equations & Inequalities 3 (p. 38)

a. (7, 14)   b. (5, -2)

Systems of Linear Equations & Inequalities 4 (p. 38)

a. (2, -1)   b. $(\frac{2}{3}, 3)$

Systems of Linear Equations & Inequalities 5 (p. 39)

a. (1, 1)   b. (3, 0)

Systems of Linear Equations & Inequalities 6 (p. 39)

a. (11, -1)   b. (2, 6)

Systems of Linear Equations & Inequalities 7 (p. 39)
a. (-3, 3) b. (3, 1)

Systems of Linear Equations & Inequalities 8 (p. 39)
a. (1, 1) b. (-4, -5)

Systems of Linear Equations & Inequalities 9 (p. 40)
a. $n = 2m + 4$ b. $a = \frac{1}{2}(b - 3)$

Systems of Linear Equations & Inequalities 10 (p. 40)
a. $S + 6 = 2R + 4$ b. $0.10d = \dfrac{0.25q}{2}$

Systems of Linear Equations & Inequalities 11 (p. 40)
a. $\begin{cases} x + y = 36 \\ x - y = 4 \end{cases}$ (20, 16)

Systems of Linear Equations & Inequalities 12 (p. 41)
a. $\begin{cases} 5n + 25q = 310 \\ n + q = 26 \end{cases}$ 17 nickels, 9 quarters

Systems of Linear Equations & Inequalities 13 (p. 41)
a. $\begin{cases} J + D = 137 \\ J = 2D - 10 \end{cases}$ José 88, Dan 49

Systems of Linear Equations & Inequalities 14 (p. 41)
a. $\begin{cases} E = M + 3 \\ E - 4 = 2(M - 4) \end{cases}$ Ella 10, Marta 7

Systems of Linear Equations & Inequalities 15 (p. 41)
a. $\begin{cases} D = 3A \\ (D + 3) + (A + 3) = 54 \end{cases}$ David 36, Alex 12

Square Roots & Radicals 1 (p. 42)
a. 7 b. ±0.9 c. $-\frac{1}{4}$ d. 30

Square Roots & Radicals 2 (p. 42)
a. ±24 b. 0.05 c. -3 d. -1.4

Square Roots & Radicals 3 (p. 42)
a. 3 b. 2 c. 4 d. -5

Square Roots & Radicals 4 (p. 42)
a. $6\sqrt{2}$ or $3\sqrt{8}$ b. $6\sqrt{3}$
c. $2\sqrt{11}$ d. $3\sqrt{10}$

Square Roots & Radicals 5 (p. 43)
a. $2\sqrt{6}$ b. $5\sqrt{6}$ c. $4\sqrt{3}$ or $2\sqrt{12}$
d. $10\sqrt{10}$

Square Roots & Radicals 6 (p. 43)
a. $2\sqrt{2}$ b. $2\sqrt{7}$ c. $3\sqrt{3}$

Square Roots & Radicals 7 (p. 43)
a. $3ab^2\sqrt{a}$ b. $\dfrac{5\sqrt{2}}{7}$ c. $\dfrac{9\sqrt{5}}{5}$ d. $\frac{5}{9}$

Square Roots & Radicals 8 (p. 43)
a. $7\sqrt{11}$ b. $4\sqrt{15}$ c. $-3\sqrt{6}$

Square Roots & Radicals 9 (p. 44)
a. $-2\sqrt{x}$ b. $3\sqrt{r}$ c. $23\sqrt{3}$

Square Roots & Radicals 10 (p. 44)
a. $x^2\sqrt{y}$ b. $9y^4\sqrt{y}$ c. b^2c^3
d. $2r^2\sqrt{22}$

Square Roots & Radicals 11 (p. 44)
a. $19\sqrt{5}$ b. $4\sqrt{n}$

Square Roots & Radicals 12 (p. 44)
a. $12\sqrt{y}$ b. 0

Square Roots & Radicals 13 (p. 45)
a. $5\sqrt{2}$ b. $-6\sqrt{6}$ c. $\sqrt{3}$

Square Roots & Radicals 14 (p. 45)
a. -7 b. $4\sqrt{7}+7$ c. $16n$

Square Roots & Radicals 15 (p. 45)
a. $\dfrac{\sqrt{2}}{2}$ b. $-\dfrac{2}{5}\sqrt{15}$ c. $\dfrac{3}{16}$

Square Roots & Radicals 16 (p. 46)
a. $\dfrac{\sqrt{6}}{2}$ b. $\dfrac{2\sqrt{2y}}{y}$ c. $2x$

Square Roots & Radicals 17 (p. 46)
a. 64 b. 12 c. $\dfrac{17}{2}$

Square Roots & Radicals 18 (p. 46)
a. 11 b. 6 c. 4

Square Roots & Radicals 19 (p. 47)
a. $b=12$ b. $a=3$ c. $c=2$

Square Roots & Radicals 20 (p. 47)
a. 5 b. 10

Quadratic Equations 1 (p. 48)
a. $(4, -3)$ b. $(0, \frac{9}{4})$ c. $(\frac{3}{2}, \frac{4}{3})$

Quadratic Equations 2 (p. 48)
a. $(-\frac{2}{3}, 5)$ b. $(0, \frac{12}{7})$ c. $(-3, \frac{2}{5})$

Quadratic Equations 3 (p. 48)
a. $\pm\dfrac{\sqrt{10}}{5}$ b. $\pm\dfrac{\sqrt{2}}{2}$ c. $\pm2\sqrt{2}$

Quadratic Equations 4 (p. 49)
a. $g=\pm7$ b. $h=\pm13$ c. $x=\pm\frac{9}{5}$

Quadratic Equations 5 (p. 49)
a. $(4, -2)$ b. $\pm2\sqrt{3}$ c. $(-1, \frac{1}{7})$

Quadratic Equations 6 (p. 49)
a. $(-2, 4)$ b. $-5\pm\sqrt{22}$ c. $\frac{3}{2}$

Quadratic Equations 7 (p. 50)
a. $\dfrac{1\pm\sqrt{5}}{2}$ b. $(-15, 3)$ c. $2\pm\sqrt{2}$

Quadratic Equations 8 (p. 50)
a. $(-1, \frac{5}{2})$ b. $(-3, -2)$

Quadratic Equations 9 (p. 50)
a. $(5, -2)$ b. $(2, 1)$

Quadratic Equations 10 (p. 50)
a. $\pm\sqrt{5}$ b. $(3, 1)$

Quadratic Equations 11 (p. 51)
a. $(0, 7)$ b. $(0, 4.5)$ c. $(-4, -2)$

Quadratic Equations 12 (p. 51)
a. $(2, 1)$ b. $(10, 6)$

Quadratic Equations 13 (p. 51)
a. $(1, -\frac{5}{2})$ b. $(4, 7)$

Quadratic Equations 14 (p. 51)
a. $(1, -\frac{4}{5})$ b. $(3, -\frac{2}{3})$